The Love Book

By John Randolph Price

Books
The Abundance Book
*Angel Energy
*The Angels Within Us
Empowerment
*Living a Life of Joy
The Love Book
The Meditation Book
Practical Spirituality
A Spiritual Philosophy for the New World
The Success Book
The Superbeings
The Wellness Book
With Wings As Eagles
The Workbook for Self-Mastery

Selected Audiocassettes
The 40-Day Prosperity Plan
A Journey into the Fourth Dimension
The Manifestation Process
Prayer, Principles & Power

Check your bookstore for the books and audios above.
All items except those with asterisks
can be ordered through Hay House:
800-654-5126 • 800-650-5115 (fax)

Please visit the Hay House Website at:
www.hayhouse.com

THE LOVE BOOK

JOHN RANDOLPH PRICE

Hay House, Inc.
Carlsbad, CA

Copyright © 1998 by John Randolph Price
Published and distributed in the United States by:
Hay House, Inc., P.O. Box 5100, Carlsbad, CA 92018-5100
(800) 654-5126 • (800) 650-5115 (fax)

Edited by: Jill Kramer
Designed by: Wendy Lutge

All rights reserved. No part of this book may be reproduced by any mechanical, photographic, or electronic process, or in the form of a phonographic recording, nor may it be stored in a retrieval system, transmitted, or otherwise be copied for public or private use—other than for "fair use" as brief quotations embodied in articles and reviews without prior written permission of the publisher.

The author of this book does not dispense medical advice or prescribe the use of any technique as a form of treatment for physical or medical problems without the advice of a physician, either directly or indirectly. The intent of the author is only to offer information of a general nature to help you in your quest for emotional and spiritual well-being. In the event you use any of the information in this book for yourself, which is your constitutional right, the author and the publisher assume no responsibility for your actions.

Library of Congress Cataloging-in-Publication Data

Price, John Randolph.
    The love book / John Randolph Price.
    p. cm.
    ISBN   1-56170-503-9 (trade paper)
    1. Spiritual life. 2. Love—Religious aspects. 3. Interpersonal relations—Religious aspects. I. Title.
BL626.4.P75   1998   98-41536
177'.7—dc21   CIP

ISBN 1-56170-503-9

01 00 99 98   4 3 2 1
First Printing, December 1998

Printed in Canada

Dedicated to those who have discovered and put into practice the final and ultimate mystery of life, the overcomer of every limitation, the energy that is the cause behind all manifestation, the power behind all creation:
Love!

Contents

Introduction ix

PART I: THE POWER OF LOVE

Chapter One: The Force of Universal Love 1

Chapter Two: All Is Love 9

Chapter Three: The Heart Center of Love 19

Chapter Four: Selected Excerpts on Love 25

PART II: LOVING RELATIONSHIPS

Chapter Five: A Story of Healing Love 43

Chapter Six: Circles of Relationships 47

Chapter Seven: There Is Only One Relationship 53

Chapter Eight: Living with Love 63

Chapter Nine: Love Reminders 73

About the Author 77

≫ INTRODUCTION

The Love Book is a compilation of my writings on love—part of a series of small volumes that began with *The Abundance Book*. Through such a consolidation of material, the reader will have the opportunity to focus on a specific topic or divine attribute for deeper understanding and expansion of consciousness. This is particularly important in the discussion of the true meaning of love.

Several years ago my "old man" (who represents the wisdom of my Higher Self) appeared to me in a dream and gave me the greatest secret in the universe. He spoke six words very slowly: *"If you would only love more . . . ,"* then added what would happen if I followed his instructions . . . *"all limitations in your life will vanish."*

Let's pause for a moment and think about that. LIMITATIONS—whether in time, finances, health, relationships, career, or any other area—would vanish, be dissolved, if I only loved more. I thought about the dream on and off for most of the following day, but by the second day I was continuing on about my business, trying to demonstrate prosperity, solve some personal problems, and figure how to squeeze a 36-hour activity into 24.

I was reminded of the dream again years later and was told that love is the most misunderstood aspect of the Cosmos—that it is the final and ultimate mystery and the highest expression of alchemy. Still later, the inner voice said that love is the Foundation Stone of the New Jerusalem. Understand that the form of love I'm referring to is not from the level of personality, but from the Soul plane. Love radiating from the Soul is not affection or sentiment—neither is it human emotion that seeks to please or possess, nor is it an impractical ideal or selfish indulgence to make one "feel good." No, the love that will transform the world (and our individual lives) cannot even be grasped in its fullness by the lower nature. It is simply too deep, intense, extreme, and profound for people living solely in third-dimensional mind and emotions.

To properly describe this "overcomer of every limitation," we must remember that there is only one universal, infinite, and eternal energy, and that is the energy of love. It is the energy that is the cause behind all manifestation, the power behind all creation—whether universes, solar systems, physical bodies, or the visible supply that we call money.

Love is the Divine Activity that impels and guides the laws of evolution, radiation, attraction, synthesis, correspondence, and transmutation. It is the spiritual vibration that carries the Divine Thought-forms from Mind into concrete expression. It is the Cosmic Fire that manipulates time, changes matter, creates new form, vivifies all things, dissolves earthly karma, and emits a fiery auric radiation that lifts up the consciousness of all in proximity to its motivating power.

Love in its highest aspect is the Force behind the Will of God, the Vision of Christ, and the Action of the Holy Spirit. It is the Alchemy that will transmute the consciousness of nations and individuals, bringing all aspects of planetary life up to the Divine Standard of spiritual wholeness.

In Part I we will probe deeply into the permanent atom of Universal Love, see how the energy of love dissolves error patterns and eliminates fear, and realize that love is the reality behind all form and the force that animates it. We will also explore the heart center and open the passageway between Heaven and Earth, understand how love is the fulfilling of the law, and train ourselves to *be* love in action. Then in Part II we will look at loving relationships and how to avail ourselves of the mighty power of unconditional love to heal and harmonize existing relationships, and how to attract and find loving fulfillment with the right partner in life.

With love, truly nothing is impossible.

PART I
The Power of Love

1

THE FORCE OF UNIVERSAL LOVE

That which we call an "individual" is in reality an energy field composed of storage cells called atoms. With every incarnation, new atoms replace the old as karmic patterns are transmuted. However, one of the Permanent Atoms within each individual's energy field is the Atom representing the centralized force of Universal Love.

Einstein's Theory of Relativity tells us that an extremely large amount of mass can be changed into a large amount of energy. The "mass" referred to is matter—not "unreal" or an illusion in mortal mind, but the smallest particle of reality found on the physical plane, the atom. The word *matter* can also be traced back to its root word of *substance*, which is the essential quality of the magnetic field of the universe.

My point is that each one of us is an energy field of atomic substance, and the power of the universe is concentrated right where we are in the physical, material world. Within each individual atomic field is the Permanent Atom of Universal Love, the One that will trigger a self-sustaining chain reaction to produce a total transformation of the individual, and ultimately the entire collective consciousness. At the nucleus or central core of this Atom is the greatest concentration of energy in the world, and this energy is released through the fission (opening) of the nuclei.

The mechanism of fission within each individual is an act of consciousness. It is being consciously aware and recognizing that you have this Permanent Atom of Universal Love right within you now—followed by the understanding that it can be opened to release its awesome force simply by loving more intensely, powerfully, and universally. Simple but not easy. The ancients said that universal love is difficult to apply to human conditions because of the selfishness of human nature. But we must begin somewhere if the sacred Atom is going to be split, and we start with love as we understand it at the present level of consciousness.

The Force of Universal Love

You begin where you are by pouring love into your immediate environment. With purpose of mind, you remove unloving thoughts from your consciousness and practice *harmlessness* in thoughts and words. You keep loving in your small circle until you can expand your love nature and truthfully say that you love everyone without exception—and that includes everyone who has ever hurt you, anyone who has ever caused you mental suffering or emotional distress, anyone who has ever pushed your button and caused a flare of resentment. You must reach the point where you can radiate unconditional love to terrorists, murderers, rapists, child abusers, religious fanatics, political extremists, and any other so-called evil individual or group. You must be detached and loving toward all!

At the same time you continue to ponder, contemplate, and meditate on this sacred Atom of Love within—seeing it magnified in your mind as a beautiful pearl, or a blazing jewel of light—and you love it with all of your being. You feel its presence in your heart, and with controlled visualization you see it slowly opening and see and feel its mighty radiation from its central core. Let that Love-Light shine through you and go before you to touch all souls, to open minds and soften hearts, to lift consciousness—and to heal, harmonize, prosper, protect, adjust, guide, strengthen, and forgive.

Practice love and loving daily as an initiate preparing for the role of Master of Love.

Then one day you will notice a decided shift in consciousness. Your love for all beings will have moved above human emotions, beyond conditional love, to an impersonal feeling of Will-for-Good for all universal life forms. And in a split second, the all-consuming Fire will engulf you. Fission will have taken place and you become radioactive—literally! The chain reaction sets in, every atom of your being is transformed, and you become a radiating Center of Universal Love.

As those Cosmic Rays flow out to touch the activities in your personal life, every aspect is healed and harmonized, and you know that nothing can ever touch you again but love. And the power grows and the radiation moves through the lower kingdoms, all people, all nations—joining with other streams of Radiance until the Energy of Universal Love permeates and saturates Planet Earth, and the world is restored to sanity.

Seven Days of Love . . . and Continuing

My wife, Jan, and I tried a seven-day experiment. We made a commitment on a particular day to begin, with purpose of mind, to love as we had never loved before—and for seven days we vowed to *be* love, *live* love, and *radiate* love with all of the power and vibrancy of our beings.

We devoted our entire meditations to love and only love, and we worked with spiritual exercises to magnify the Love Atom and open it. We poured love into every situation that had the potential to pull on our consciousness, into every person we met or thought about, into all forms of life on this planet and beyond, and into the infinite reaches of the universe—all on an hour-by-hour, day-to-day basis.

On the third day, I awoke hearing myself blessing with universal love the masculine and feminine energies throughout the infinite worlds, so it was obvious that a deeper level of consciousness had taken over even when I was asleep. By the fifth day, the radiation was so intense that it was felt during most of my waking hours. I should also mention that during that week, we experienced more peace, contentment, and divine order than we can ever remember.

But there was more. Time seemed to work in our favor as we accomplished so much more in less time. Relationships with everyone took on a deeper meaning, visible supply moved to a higher level, guidance dreams were of greater frequency and clarity, and the vision of our purpose expanded considerably. Love is truly the Final and Ultimate Mystery . . . the greatest secret in the universe.

A Meditation

Relax and let go. Be still in mind and emotions, and bring the focus of your attention to your heart center where the Permanent Atom of Universal Love is located. Say to yourself:

*I am love, I am loved, I am loving.
I feel the love vibration in my heart . . . I feel
it expanding throughout my body. All there is,
is love . . . love . . . love . . . love.*

In your mind's eye, see the Atom of Universal Love in your heart center. Imagine it as a shining Crystal of Love, a glistening Jewel of Love. Contemplate it. Focus on the Love Diamond with clarity of vision, and know that all the love in the universe is concentrated right there, within you. Now, in your imagination see it slowly open to release its light. See the radiant rays begin to flow, moving and filling your entire energy field . . . your mind, your feelings, your body. See yourself as a radiating Center of Divine Love. See the Love Essence

The Force of Universal Love

radiating and filling the room where you are, continuing to flow in streams of Golden Light . . . moving out across the land to encircle this planet. See the radiance of your Permanent Atom of Universal Love flowing like a mighty stream, and see this world filled with the Light of Love. Now say to yourself:

I am Universal Love in radiant expression, and I now love as I have never loved before in my life. I silently, powerfully, and intensely radiate my love, and I send it everywhere without exception. I see it flowing into my family and my loved ones. I see the Cosmic Rays of Love going before me to envelop and permeate everyone in my consciousness.

Those who have rejected me, who have hurt me, who have not recognized my true worth, I send my love to you with no conditions attached. I love you for Who and What you are. I love everyone without exception. I love everything without exception. I am the mighty power of God's love in radiant expression, and I let my love go before me to heal and harmonize every condition in my life.

Spirit of the Living God within, I am your love. I am your love in expression, and I will keep this love vibration in my heart, and thoughts of love in my mind, moment by moment, hour by hour, day by day, for I know that as I begin to love more and more, every limitation in my life will vanish, and my personal world will become whole and joyous.

And the Light is growing and spreading. My Light of Love is joining with others who have opened the Crystal of Love, and together we are saturating this world with love. The healing has begun, it is happening now, and I am doing my part to dissolve the limitations of humankind and restore this world to sanity.

I love as I have never loved before. I can love because I know Who and What I am. I am love, and I will never hold back my love. I will let it forever flow unconditionally, universally, divinely, powerfully, intensely.

I am love, and I rest now in the silence, thinking only of the love I am, and the love I give, and the love I receive.

All there is, is love.

2
ALL IS LOVE

If your life is not overflowing with abundance, wellness, and fulfillment, you are out of tune with the Love Vibration within you. If you want more out of life, you are going to have to give more to life. When you give more love, you receive the Kingdom.

Love is what created the universe, and Love is what the universe was created out of. Therefore, Love is Mind and also the thoughts of Mind. Love is the thrust of all creation. "And God said . . . " And the Word was Love, and the Power of the Word was Love, and the manifestation of the Power was Love. All *is* Love!

The Infinite All is the pure essence of Love. This Infinite Love thinks. Its Consciousness is perfect Love.

As It contemplates Itself, It does so with Love. And what It sees, It loves. This Father-Mother Mind conceived the perfect Image of Love, which became the first Principle, the ever-living male and female Principle, the I AM THAT I AM, the Love-Self-Reality of each one of us.

In the beginning, you knew only love. And your creations of materiality were born out of love, for you were a co-creator with God, bringing forth into manifestation only the Divine Ideas of Love. But once you began to identify yourself with your creations, you sealed off the Love Vibration with a material consciousness. Yet you continued to be, and always will be, a spiritual being of Love.

Some men and women have rediscovered (awakened to) their true nature of Love and have opened the inner door to receive once again the Energy of Love, letting it fill their consciousness and eliminate the error patterns of the past as light dissolves darkness. I call these people Superbeings.

Are you one? If you are, you know that you are Spirit, that Spirit is Love, and that Love is the activity of Spirit. You know that the Activity of Spirit is Its Self-expression, and since your conscious awareness of Spirit is that Self-expression, you are pure Love. You know that the Love that created you forever sustains you.

Knowing that the Spirit of God—*your* Spirit—loves Its expression as your Personality, you relax and let the burdens fall from your shoulders. Say to yourself:

Since the only Presence and Power of the Universe loves me and sustains me, what on earth could I possibly fear? Nothing. No-thing. Love heals, Love prospers, Love protects, Love guards, Love guides, Love restores, Love creates, Love makes all things new. So I let Love go before me now to straighten out every crooked place in my life. I place my faith in God's Love for me, and I am free, as I was created to be.

Your God-Self will restore your life and transform your world into a Garden of peace, joy, beauty, abundance, and fulfillment. But remember, you are a co-creator with God—not just an empty projector through which images are thrown on the screen of your world. You have a role to play, too, and that role is to be a conscious participant as a radiating center of Divine Love.

Your *center*—which is another word for your energy field—includes thoughts, feelings, words, and deeds. Therefore, to be a co-creator with the Spirit of Love, you must think love, feel love, speak love, and act with love. Your first thought of love should be to respond to the love that your God-Self is eternally pouring out upon you. Since this Presence within you loves you with all of Its Divine Consciousness, should you not reciprocate by loving this Reality of you with all your mind, your heart, and your strength? Can you not express gratitude for that love by returning the love in full measure? When you do, the Connection is restored, and the middle wall of partition is blown away.

Turn within and say:

> *Thank you for loving me. Regardless of what I have done in the past, I know that your love for me has never diminished. Even when I ignored you or blamed you or took action contrary to your counsel, you continued to love me with all of your Being. I love your Love! And I love You! My heart runneth over with love for You, my Friend, my Guide, my Wonderful One, my Counselor, my mighty God, my everlasting Father, my Prince of Peace, my very Christ Self. Love is what I have received, and love is what I give, and I am now whole and complete.*

Since this God Presence within you *is* you—the Higher Self of you—and since this Self is forever expressing as the allness of you, can you now begin to love *all* of you from center to circumference? There is no place where God leaves off and you begin, so all is God, and all is you. *Know Thyself!* To know yourself is to love yourself—all the way through. And do not think that you are not worthy, because your worthiness is God's Worthiness. *Love Thyself!*

Think beautiful thoughts about yourself:

I am a delightful Child of God. My Spirit is God being me in the absolute. My conscious awareness of the indwelling Presence—my illumined personality—is God being me in expression. My body is God being me in physical form. I am God being me!

Knowing that everything I have ever done, ever said, ever thought, and ever felt was simply my consciousness in action, I understand that I could not have expressed any differently. I was acting out of my consciousness; therefore, I dismiss all thoughts of right and wrong. That was simply where I was at the time, and I know now that my consciousness is evolving and I am returning Home to the Light of Love.

So I no longer condemn me. I no longer hold any unforgiveness toward myself. I rise above all feelings of guilt, and I am free to love myself as never before. I love this person I am with all my mind. I love this Individual I am with all my heart. My love for me, myself, the I that I AM, knows no bounds. I am Love. I am Love. I am Love.

You are told to love your neighbor as yourself, and your "neighbor" means every other soul on this planet and beyond and all forms of life throughout the universe. So now, turn your attention to the world and begin to radiate the Love Rays. When you direct the beams from the Love Energy Center of your heart, they go before you to transform every negative situation your neighbor may be experiencing into a splendid positive. This is Power-Love, rather than cuddly, fuzzy love; and there is nothing it cannot do. When you direct it toward anyone or anything, it literally changes the energy field in and around the person, place, or thing. This is God in action, peeling away the illusion and revealing the Reality.

Say to yourself:

I will do my part to love my neighbor without exception. As I scan my consciousness, my mind picks up certain individuals of the past and present who evoke less-than-desirable emotions in me. I now transmute that negative energy by forgiving them and speaking words of unconditional love.

(Speak the name aloud) . . . *I love you! I love you unconditionally! I love you for Who and What you are with no strings attached. I am love. You are love. We are one in love, and we are healed through love.*

I now bring into my consciousness my home and family, my place of work, my city, state, and country, my world—and I send forth the Love Rays to heal and harmonize every negative condition on this planet. I feel the love pouring forth from my heart center, and I know that this Love Power will accomplish that for which it is sent. I am Love in Action!

Spend time daily with the affirmative prayers in this chapter, then continue to be Love in action. *Be* God in action! Do not get caught in the mesmerism of listening and watching others fight, fume, and spew negative energy. Begin to pour love into the situation from your heart chakra, radiating it with intensity, and joyfully watch as the individuals are touched by the harmonizing rays. If injustice comes within the range of your consciousness, send forth the spiritual Energy of Love and see right action taking place. Use the Love Power in your home, your office, in the grocery store, the restaurants, the hospitals, the courtrooms, on the freeways—and notice how the environment changes. Stop being a spectator. Use your Love Rays in the service of Godkind to reveal order, harmony, and peace in this world.

Practice the use of Love-Power daily, and prove to yourself that you do indeed have a divine "zapper" at your disposal. If an insect bites you, focus the love energy at the point of contact and feel the instant relief from the sting. If you meet someone in a bad mood, throw open your heart and begin to pour out unconditional love with great purpose of mind, and watch as darkness changes to light. You can love a failing business back to life. You can love a diseased body back to wellness. And you can love a negative condition right out of existence.

The act (feeling) of unconditional love opens the heart chakra and propels the harmonizing energy directly into the low vibratory force field and begins to "perk up" the vibration, literally lifting it to the Divine Standard. If you will just practice the procedure, you will be amazed at the results. Don't just think about it—do it!

When you are not purposely using your Love-Power, continue to *be* the Presence of Love. For example, can the Presence of Love experience hurt feelings? Can Individualized Love feel rejected? Does a Master of Love attack out of anger? Would a Being of Love feel bitterness or resentment? Would God's perfect expression of Love condemn or criticize? You know the answers. Begin to live as the Love you are in Truth.

You might also spend some time in meditation reflecting on what Paul said about love in his letter to the Christians at Corinth:

> *If I speak with the eloquence of men and of angels, but have no love, I become no more than blaring brass or crashing cymbals. If I have the gift of foretelling the future and hold in my mind not only all human knowledge but the very secrets of God, and if I also have that absolute faith which can move mountains, but I have no love, I amount to nothing at all. If I dispose of all that I possess, yes, even if I give my own body to be burned, but have no love, I achieve nothing.*
>
> *This love of which I speak is slow to lose patience—it looks for a way of being constructive. It is not possessive: It is neither*

anxious to impress nor does it cherish inflated ideas of its own importance.

Love has good manners and does not pursue selfish advantage. It is not touchy. It does not keep account of evil or gloat over the wickedness of other people. On the contrary, it is glad with all good men when truth prevails.

Love knows no limit to its endurance, no end to its trust, no fading of its hope; it can outlast anything. It is, in fact, the one thing that still stands when all else has fallen.

3

THE HEART CENTER OF LOVE

When the Truth of Who and What we really are begins to dawn in us, those first faint rays of recognition are felt in the heart, and the birthing process commences, leading ultimately to the fusion of the Self and the personality.

What is meant by the *heart*? The Bible has 169 references to "heart"—and in the Ancient Wisdom literature, the heart is considered to be of extraordinary importance. Are the mystics and masters referring to the physical organ? No, for the body is not the cause of anything. Are they pointing to our emotional system? No, the etheric center (chakra) corresponding to the solar plexus is the instrument through which the emotional energy flows. Are they talking about our feeling nature? To some extent, yes, but the major emphasis is on an energy center that is the source of the most awesome power of the universe.

The heart center is the fourth or middle chakra in the chain of seven located within the lines of force that make up the etheric body. Where the lines of force cross each other, they form great "whirlpools" for the distribution of energy. And each of the seven major centers receives a *specialized* energy from the Central Core of Being, the Master Self, for circulation through the individual's Force Field. The heart chakra is considered the "Agent" of Self, and serves as the outlet for the extension of energy into the phenomenal world and the manifestation of form. Whatever we consider good, true, and beautiful in life must come through the heart center if it is to have any degree of permanency in our individual worlds. It is also the focal point where emotions are transmuted into the feelings of unconditional love, and it is the place where the "Christ Idea" of our Divine Identity is born. This is the first initiation into higher consciousness, the acceptance of our Truth of Being.

What are we to do to avail ourselves of this passageway between Heaven and Earth? First, we should understand the dynamics of this Power Center. We are told in the Bible that "the Lord looks on the heart"

(1 Sam. 17:7). This means that the focus of our Holy Self is on this "lotus" in a concentrated gaze of loving knowingness. "And I will give them one heart, and put a new spirit within them" (Ex. 11:19). "I will put my law within them, and I will write it upon their hearts" Jer. 31:33). Here we see that within the vortex where the powers of God unite and spirit and matter join is the *universal* production facility for everything that appears in our lives. And it is under the direction of the "new spirit" —"new" because it is the nature of our Self being reborn. This Spirit of Truth formed in us represents the law of the Lord-Self—"law" being the spiritual principles of life that are impressed (written) on the heart.

And let's remember that "as he thinketh in his heart, so is he" (Prov. 23:7). When we think with the heart, with thoughts clothed in love, we are in tune with the Higher Mind—"I commune with my heart in the night" (Ps. 77:6). How do we bring in that Higher Mind to dramatically transform our world? By meditating on the Great Self within, which connects us with the Gaze and fills our heart center with the Truth that sets us free.

In this regard, think of the heart as a circle of light that expands with every degree of Self recognition, ever enlarging to accommodate more and more of the Divine Incarnation. If we just *talk* about our Inner Reality all the time, the problems and challenges will continue to be concretized. But as we become truly *conscious* of the Indwelling Presence, things begin to happen, and with every step we take in consciousness toward the Ultimate Merger, the faster and more complete is the transformation.

Let your Holy Self be formed in your heart. As you contemplate the Divine Presence, more of that Presence is formed in the substance of this Power Center. This is the new Birth; it is being born anew. This is the Kingdom that comes, the Daily Bread that satisfies every hunger. At first it is only a child in the manger, only a light of the Kingdom, a small slice of the Bread of Life. But in this child is all the power of God, in that light is the Sun of Miracles, and in that slice is eternal manna from Heaven.

Fill your heart with a conscious awareness of your Master Self as the answer to every problem, the fulfillment of every need—as the Source, Energy, and Activity of every form, condition, situation, and experience in your life. And as that recognition builds in the Love Center and radiates out to encompass your world, you will see it as it was in the beginning—a time of wholeness, abundance, joy, and peace.

Begin now. Look within and feel the radiant splendor of your Lord Self reaching down and touching your Love Center, and bow your head to the point of that feeling and behold the Wonder Child. Cross your arms over your heart, and pay homage to this Magnificent One Who heals all your infirmities, casts out the demons of ego, feeds the multitudes, stills the tempest, provides the money for the Tribute, and turns the waters of negation into the fruits of a life more abundant. Express your love for this Angel of the Presence, and make a commitment now to care for this Light of your world with devoted attention and overflowing love.

A Meditation

> *Spirit of the living God within, my Spirit, my very God-Self . . . my heart overflows with love for you. My Soul sings songs of boundless adoration for you . . . my mind reaches out to you in total devotion . . . and I radiate the love I am and have to you with all the power of my being. Oh, I love you so much! You are all I seek, and nothing in my life is more important than my oneness with you.*

Now in the silence, listen as Love speaks of love.

4

SELECTED EXCERPTS ON LOVE

Hooking Up with the Energy of Love

When will is brought into alignment with love, your vision becomes broader and your consciousness is lifted into a higher vibration. You continue to move toward your objective, but that objective now includes freedom, joy, peace, abundance, wholeness, and happiness—not only for yourself, but for all humanity. The drive of will combined with the energy of love from the heart center makes you a Lightbearer—a blessing to everyone within the range of your consciousness. Also, the will-to-Good (the unity of will and love) will eliminate spiritual inertia, will lift your gaze

THE LOVE BOOK

above the purely physical world, and will transform absolute passivity into spiritual action.

Try this exercise with me. First, see with your inner eye a vertical beam of light connecting the love faculty in your heart to the power of will in the high center of your forehead. Let your awareness and feelings run up and down the beam. As you inhale, move with the Light from the heart up to the head; as you exhale, move down the beam of Light from the head to the heart. Breathe deeply as you practice the connecting of these two powers, devoting two or three minutes to the exercise.

Next, concentrate on your heart center, and say with deep feeling:

I love the Self I was created to be.

Now place your attention on the high center of your forehead, and say with great strength of will and purpose of mind:

**I am determined to realize the Self
that I was created to be.**

Down to the heart with feeling:

I love my Self.

Up to the head with firmness and power:

**I now make the conscious decision
to be my Self.**

Down to the heart:

Selected Excerpts on Love

>   **I love every Soul on this planet
>   and beyond as my Self.**

Up to the head:

>   **I choose wholeness and harmony
>   for everyone without exception.**

Down to the heart:

>   **I love this world.**

Up to the head:

>   **I am determined to do my part as
>   a healing channel.**

Down to the heart:

>   **I love the activity of Spirit in my
>   life and in the lives of all others.**

Up to the head:

>   **I am the activity of Spirit as a
>   distributor of God Power.**

Down to the heart:

>   **I love my mission in life.**

Up to the head:

>   **I now go forth with great enthusiasm
>   to accomplish that which Spirit has
>   for me to do.**

The uniting of these two powers will balance your energies, start your "engine," and press the accelerator to give you the go-power to move toward your destination with loving determination. By connecting the powers of love and will and expressing them in your daily life, you will receive all the inspiration, guidance, and enthusiasm you need to chart your course, pull up the anchor, and move out to find your piece of the puzzle. And as you do, you'll notice those "challenges" falling away and vanishing from your life because you will be moving out of the low vibration of the lower self where problems find entrance into your life and affairs.

Use your will to build a fire under you and to get your momentum going—and let love point the way and be the guiding light to the mountaintop.

A Love Affair with Self

Love the Presence of God within you, your Spirit, with all your heart, with all your soul, with all your mind, and with all your strength.

When you contemplate that Presence within, your very Spirit, with great love, that one-pointed love-focus will literally draw the awesome and incredible power of the universe right into your thinking mind and feeling nature. You take on the Power and you become the

Power and you speak as the Power—and behold—all things are made new!

Jesus called this the first and greatest of all the commandments because of the effect of this activity on consciousness, and if there ever was a "magic formula" for turning our personal worlds right-side-up, this is it. Meditating on your Presence with all the love you can feel in your entire being changes the vibration of your energy field and moves you to a higher frequency faster than anything I can think of. And in the process, you are disconnected from the race consciousness, and false beliefs and error patterns are burned away by the fire of the Living Christ.

But this is not something you do once or twice a day. The secret is to *live* that Love of the Presence . . . to glance within many times a day and express your adoration . . . to court your Holy Self with total interest and attention.

Find your point of contact, and begin the Love Affair this very day. That point may be the feeling of love in your heart, a Light seen with the inner eye, or perhaps an awareness in your mind of a higher Presence hovering in the background of your consciousness. Find that focal point—identify it as your connection with your Master Self—and pour all the love you can feel into it. Do it now.

Love and Money

Ageless Wisdom teaches us that money is the energy of divinity, and that in fulfilling our needs we must work with the energy of love and not desire. I have found that if I somehow shut down the Love Vibration—the feeling of complete unconditional love for everyone—I am putting a heavy restriction on my visible supply.

Remember that our "natural energy" is love; therefore, the "yield" is created out of love and returns to us on wings of love. Without the intense radiation of love, there simply cannot be the full and complete manifestation and attraction of supply-in-form.

Love, a Part of the Manifestation Process

While you are visualizing your good, be sure to *love* what you see. Pour all the love you have into those finished pictures—generate that warm, passionate, and powerful feeling of love; and let it radiate through those images in your mind. Remember that Love Energy is the most powerful force in the universe, the power behind the whole thrust of creation, and that Love Power will clothe your images with radiant substance for perfect manifestation in the phy-sical world.

Substance is the creative energy of everything visible, the divine idea underlying all physical manifestation. When you consciously radiate the energy of love, when with purpose of mind you send forth currents of love through your mental pictures, when you love what you see with deep-deep feeling, you are propelling the substance and giving it a clear path to follow as it moves from cause into effect. Substance is the raw material out of which everything visible is formed, and love is the animating force that forms it.

When you love what you see with all your heart, your mental images will stand out with great clarity and will become *real* (substantial) to you. Through the love vibration, you unite the conscious, subconscious, and Superconscious phases of your mind, and you truly embody the pattern that represents the fulfillment of your desires. Love power will help you to realize the truth of that which you are seeking—and this realization must, by law, outpicture itself in your world. As above, so below. As within, so without.

> *Oh how I love what I see. I love the joyous expressions and the happy scenes. I love doing what I love to do. I love being what I want to*

be. I love having what I want to have. I love the pictures of total fulfillment that I am now seeing in my mind and feeling in my heart.

Unconditional Love

In much of the literature incorporating the teachings of ancient wisdom, the first expression, or outpouring, of Supreme Being is said to be Love, which became the Force and Energy of Creative Power.

The Force and Energy of Unconditional Love is totally and completely free, while the conditional love of human nature tends to confine and restrict both the loved one and the lover himself. The human personality, in its desire to be loved, will attempt to evoke this emotion in others, but it loves in order to be loved—the strings are eternally attached—which produces an obligation in others to meet selfish motives. Such love is manipulative and binding, whereas unconditional Love is open and without bounds. Since the time of our "fall" into material consciousness, it has not been human nature to love unconditionally, yet that is the only love that our divine soul knows.

You will know that Universal Love is flowing freely in and through you by the total absence of fear, guilt, and any feelings of repression and restriction in consciousness. If you are experiencing these negative feelings, it means that you are screening out the divine influence, specifically through the act of judging other people and conditions *based on appearances.* Let's take a closer look at what this means.

Anything that is seen as solid and tangible in the physical world—either now or imagined as coming into view at some point in the future—is an appearance. In the spiritual sense, it is an "illusion" because it is subject to change. It has a beginning and an end; therefore, it is an effect. And the only power in an effect is the power given it by the observer in the course of judging.

Look at anything in the material world, including your body. All is energy manifesting as matter. If you judge by the appearance of shortages, sickness, risks, intimidation, and danger, you are passing sentence on yourself. You are arresting the Power of Love and Freedom and are calling for even more menacing illusions appearing as substantial. The secret is to move back in consciousness, away from that which is seen, and up to the underlying energy pattern, the vibrational vortex that is constantly pulling matter into it. And where is that pattern, that vortex? Right within your consciousness. Within the living force field called *you* is the pattern for everything that exists in the phenomenal world—including the ideal relationships.

These patterns, or divine ideas, are like slides in a projector. As the Light-Energy radiates through the slide, the perfect image is projected onto the outer screen of your world, and your life appears "filled full." However, if you are experiencing an insufficiency in any area, it simply means that you have replaced the tray of divine slides with those of your own creation. And this came about by identifying yourself more with effects that seem limiting, rather than Cause, which is your unlimited consciousness.

The divine slides are waiting to be placed in the projector. Understand that *you* are the projector—your consciousness is the thing that projects. And the creative energy is flowing continuously through your consciousness, so your work now is to see (with the inner eye) the reality of the patterns, to love them with all your heart and mind, and to feel the energy pouring through the patterns and radiating out to gather matter and become substantial.

Every time you see an appearance in your world that seems to be below the divine standard of harmony, wholeness, and all-sufficiency, withdraw your attention from the outer scene and change the inner slide from an image of fear to the perfect pattern of Reality. *Change the slide!* Keep that phrase in mind, and tell it to yourself whenever that blip of fear pops in. Then contemplate the Pattern of Reality, see it securely in place in your heart center, your feeling nature, and ponder that master blueprint with total interest and love.

The Relationship Pattern, for example, is filled with convergence points for meeting the right person, for attracting only loving and harmonious people into your life, for healing all individual conflicts of the past and present, for making the right decisions regarding interaction with others, and for choosing the right mate.

There is a pattern for everything that you could possibly need or desire in this lifetime, so if you see something "out there" that has even the slightest possibility of producing fear, *change the slide!* And know that each time you do this, you are not only replacing illusion with Reality, you are also freeing the Angel of Unconditional Love and Freedom to do its mighty work of helping you realize your divine identity.

Meditations on Love

God is Love. I feel Love in my heart and know that this is the very Spirit of God flowing through my feeling nature. I could not love without God. I love; therefore, I am one with God. My understanding of God is growing.

The one all-Intelligent Power of the Universe is around and in and through me at this very moment. This Infinite Love is right now healing my body, prospering my affairs, harmonizing my relationships, giving me every good gift, adjusting all conditions, straightening out every crooked place, perfecting all that concerns me, and totally protecting me from all harm and from every negative influence.

Oh my God . . . this is really happening to me right now! And it's happening because You love me! The Power of the Universe is in love with me! And oh how I love you! The Bond of Love is complete and the sense of separation is gone. I believe this totally. I believe this completely. All darkness is gone. There is now only the Light of absolute belief. And through this perfect belief in God, every cell of my body has been renewed, the creative substance has manifested as my abundant supply, and unconditional love has permeated my world. Oh Christ, it has happened! I feel it! I know it!

The Universe is for me! God loves me! I don't have to fight anymore. There is nothing to fear anymore. It is done . . . and it is so!

💖 💖 💖

You are my beloved Self, and when I look within and feel and see and know you, I am beholding the Truth of all. Every person who has ever been a part of my consciousness is in Reality none other than you. I understand this, and now I can love everyone as my Self, for I see my Self in all, as all. My relationships of the past, present, and future are now enfolded in love and harmonized for the good of all.

The Voice of the Holy Self Speaks of Love

You have heard that love is the fulfilling of the law. It is also the way of attaining the Experience. Understand that I am the pure essence of love, and my love for you is my eternal Gift to you. As you receive my love and accept it, I become real to you. The shadows flee, the old is made new, and your life is transformed according to the level of the realization.

To receive this Gift, you must reach deeply within for it, and it must be your love that reaches out to me and for me. This is the meaning of "Give and you shall receive." You must first open the channel to receive. The Gift for you is love. To receive the Gift of Love, you must give love.

Think of two hands reaching out to touch. This is symbolic of our rays of love coming together. At the moment of contact, I am realized. Now do you see why the greatest commandment is to love me? To love me is to make the connection. To make the connection is to realize my presence. Love unceasingly.

୧ ୧ ୧

There is a Fountain of Love within you, and from it flows the fulfillment of all you could desire, the light substance to bring every form into visibility. The Fountain is never in disrepair . . . its operation is eternally perfect and its power source is my love for you, a love so great that it is beyond your comprehension.

The flow from the Fountain is endless and bountiful. Will you not stand in the stream with me now and eradicate all appearances of lack in your life? Come to me, come within and feel the rushing waters of infinite supply. Indeed your cup runneth over. There is no emptiness in my universe, no shortages, no limitations.

༘ ༘ ༘

All is forever filled full. Can you understand that I am the Fountain, the Flow, and the Fulfillment? Can you now interpret this as the Source, the Cause, and the Effect?

Now consider this, for it is very important. There is something between me and your phenomenal world. It is your consciousness. Your world mirrors that which is closest to it; therefore, your world is reflecting your consciousness. If you would have your world reflect my nature of loving sufficiency, I must be brought into your consciousness—even to the outer rim, so to speak. There, I stand before your world and the Truth is revealed. No good thing is then withheld from you. But you must not direct or prescribe the way. I am the way. Leave it in my hands. Be as a little child in joyful anticipation, keeping your thoughts on me, caring not and trusting me, fearing not and loving me. I am the Way!

PART II
Loving Relationships

❦ 5

A Story of Healing Love

Somewhere, sometime, each one of us amasses enough hostile energy in consciousness to release a silent but highly explosive force that functions just like a boomerang. And frequently we are not aware that the violent discharge has taken place because the pressure builds up gradually over a period of time and is released on a level beyond our sensory apparatus. In fact, as the malevolent thought-form moves past the final ring of consciousness, we may even feel a sense of relief followed by a stroke of "good fortune" in our lives. But on the astral plane, the thought-form is streaking toward its culminating point and will one day make the return voyage to its maker.

Just like a homing pigeon, the thought-form will someday come home to roost. In truth, this dark energy will return to us to be transmuted, and if it's not, it will continue to come back into our lives at the most unexpected time. This energy is eternal and cannot be destroyed, so it seeks to be changed back into its original state of unadulterated pureness. That's our job, and no one else can assume the responsibility for us. Let me give you an example in the story of Harry.

Harry walked through the dark night of the soul in his younger years, followed by two marriages that didn't work out and rejection by certain family members, all of which took its toll in terms of consciousness depression. You could say that Harry's point of vulnerability was relationships, and in his trial-and-error search for the "right" woman and a loving companion, there were many disappointments—each leading to a greater sense of rejection, a feeling of loss, and a hypersensitivity to criticism.

As this misdirected energy began to take hold in consciousness, a thought-form developed based on the side of rebellion and a sense of separation—a feeling of being disconnected from everything and everyone Harry thought was "good" in life. Perhaps unconsciously, he began to suspect people—and the pressure started building. Seeing others enjoying life while he was filled with despair soon ejected the thought-form out with a silent blast.

For a time, things seemed to clear up, but the thought-form had other plans for Harry. Destructive thought-forms like to magnify an individual's point of vulnerability, and in Harry's case, that point was disconnection, dissociation, separation—the antithesis of relationship. But since Harry was already playing his part in the disconnect process, the thought-form simply ensured a more visible manifestation of separation. And what better way than through an accident, which would remove Harry from his work and the daily activities of his life.

Because Harry was on the spiritual path and working with consciousness, the first fall down the stairs resulted in only a few bruises. But the destructive thought-form wasn't transmuted. It only rested a spell, gathered strength, and went out again—this time to return as an automobile accident when a drunk driver "just happened" to swerve on to Harry's side of the road. Result: No serious injuries, but a totaled car. Less than a year later, Harry fell again, ending up in the hospital with a fractured leg.

But Harry was far enough along with his spiritual studies by now to know that the cause of those accidents had to be within him. And he remembered that all things could be changed by the power of love, that a negative situation could be loved right out of existence, that misqualified energy could be transmuted through love—so Harry went to work.

He began to pour all the love he could muster in his heart into the present situation—the circumstances surrounding the accident, the broken leg, and his stay in the hospital. Then he went back in mind as far as he could remember, and with an open heart and purpose of mind, began to love and forgive his childhood, his parents, all of his so-called unhappy experiences, the failed marriages, the estrangements from family and friends, and all the other accidents. He radiated love into every negative situation, condition, circumstance, experience, and emotion. For hour after hour, day after day, Harry radiated the energy of love. Harry loved so much that he became love in expression.

It's been over a year since Harry's last accident. And during that period, he found and married a lovely and loving woman, a gentle soul who sees Harry as "the most loving man I've ever known"—a warm, caring, trusting, assured man who now treasures the oneness of his universal family.

The old thought-form? It died somewhere out on the astral plane and was resurrected as one of Harry's many thought-forms of love.

~≉~ 6
CIRCLES OF RELATIONSHIPS

Think of a target with its various circles, with impersonal, universal love for all as the outer circle. Let's move in now to the next circle and look at the wide range of our acquaintances. In this band of love, an encounter gives us the opportunity to silently salute the Holiness within the person while expressing kindness, goodwill, respect, patience, and harmlessness toward the personality—regardless of what has previously taken place in the relationship. We must forgive in the larger circles if we're going to find fulfillment as we move in toward the center.

The next space on our target is the family arena, our most difficult training ground. Prior to incarnation, we choose our parents, and our children choose us—primarily for the lessons to be learned in working off karma from past lives. The compensation is usually satisfied by age 21, and the only ties among family members at that time should be mutual love and respect, or the continuing of a close relationship based on the bonds of friendship that have been developed. For parents to hold on to their adult children is against the law of nature, and those offspring who live their lives primarily for their parents are compromising their spiritual integrity.

In the next circle, we find our friends, which may include certain members of our family. Our friends are those who accept us as we are. True friendship is a sharing relationship, a uniting in mutual understanding, where every opportunity is taken to contribute to each other's well-being. When a friendship is based not on what we can get but on what we can give, the karmic plates are positively etched with lasting compensation.

The next circle of love is our intimate, personal relationship where twin flames burn as one. There is a special ingredient that makes a significant difference in this love bond. It is *passion*. Passion in this context means deep feelings of love and ecstasy, fire in the heart, spirit, excitement, and devotion. When we're with the right person, we feel this way—not only about her or him, but also about life itself.

Circles of Relationships

I've had the great fortune of being married for over 40 years to a woman who exudes passion, and who has drawn it out in me to the point where everything in life is a glorious adventure. Perhaps the secret to our uniting as one is that we think of the other person's happiness first. Jan's joy becomes my joy and vice versa—and both of us love to play together and do things "just for the fun of it." Of course, it helps that we've been a team in many incarnations, so we've had plenty of time to get our acts together.

It's interesting that when my family moved to another town after my sophomore year in high school, our new home was only a couple of blocks from where Jan lived. I didn't pay much attention to her because she was going into eighth grade at the time and was "only a little kid." That perception was soon to change.

A few years later, I was in the U.S. Air Force stationed in Europe, and Jan was in college in Texas. I had made plans to come home on a 40-day leave. My mother gave an open house for me, and Jan came over with some friends. When our eyes met across the crowded room, we knew that we'd found each other again. We dated every night, and on Christmas Eve I told her that I loved her. She said she loved me, too. In June 1953, Jan and I were married. We spent our honeymoon and our first year of marriage in Germany.

We embarked on our spiritual journey in 1967, and I know that this search for Truth together has deepened and intensified our passion for one another, for love and life, and for God. In the adventure of growing spiritually, we found that center circle of love—the "bull's-eye."

If you have an unceasing longing for a life partner, it is because you have something special to give to someone—that which the other person is seeking and wants very much. He or she also has a rare gift for you, a quality that will make you feel complete. Here is a meditation that will help you tune into that energy of love—the attracting power of the universe:

Today I send love to this world, and I call everyone my friend regardless of who they are or what they have done, for I see only the Spirit of God in every person, including myself.

I love the Completeness I AM, the Selfhood of God we all share as our eternal Reality. I look within to this magnificent Self, and I say, I love you with all my heart, with all my soul, with all my mind, with all my strength. And I love all my neighbors on Earth as I love my Self, for we are one.

Circles of Relationships

I love unconditionally. I give my love freely, and that love returns to me in bountiful measure. I am worthy of love, of being loved, and I accept the love of others.

I think of all the people I know by name, and I feel the harmlessness and harmony that exists between us.

I look at my family unit, and I see only the expression of love, goodwill, kindness, and respect among all members.

I am thankful for my friends, and I see our relationships deepening in love, joy, and mutual understanding.

And I know there is a special Someone with overflowing love to share, who right at this moment is being attracted to the love I have to give, two flames soon uniting as one in a bond of love and ecstasy.

Love is everything. Oh how I love Love.

7
There Is Only One Relationship

While meditating on the subject of loving relationships one day, I was told to "think about relationships as applying to the bond of harmlessness and harmony between each and every individual." Of course! Loving relationships mean more than just attracting the right soulmate or finding the recipe for living with someone without conflict, for true bonding must include the entire planetary family. And when I asked what the foundation stone was for any kind of relationship, the reply was "Responsibility—the ability to respond to that which is needed by another without undermining the responsibility that is his or hers to shoulder. This is the key to Right Relations."

This tells us that if two people are going to enjoy a relationship—any kind of relationship—friends, lovers, husband and wife, father and son or daughter, mother and son or daughter, people in the workplace—all parties must be responsible. And this responsibility includes the understanding of what is required for a quality bonding and then responding fully to those needs. Yet this is to be done without violating free will and by not taking away the opportunity for the other person to grow physically, emotionally, mentally, and spiritually. Let's remember that each one of us came in with a soul assignment, and we must not take the other person's place in the School of Life and try to master the lessons for him or her. To take on another's tests under your name is cosmic cheating and will incur karma for all concerned.

A few years ago, I heard a mystic say that the creed for the new world must be "We are one, and I am responsible for you." And a friend once said that the ancient meaning of Christ is "to give what is needed." Now we can understand the significance of "responsibility"—the quality of being responsible without meddling so that we can focus on giving that which is needed. But all that we really have to give anyone are the fruits of our own consciousness, which means that once again, the starting point in any right and loving relationship is the individual you see in the mirror.

There Is Only One Relationship

First of all, we cannot truly love another person if we do not love ourselves, and this truth is emphasized and explained in Mark 12:28-31. "And one of the scribes came up and heard them disputing with one another, and seeing that he answered them well, asked him, 'Which commandment is the first of all'? Jesus answered, 'The first is, Hear, O Israel: The Lord our God, the Lord is one; and you shall love the Lord your God with all your heart, and with all your soul, and with all your mind, and with all your strength. The second is this, You shall love your neighbor as yourself. There is no other commandment greater than these.'"

Jesus tells us that "the Lord is one," meaning that the divine consciousness, the Master Self, is the one Self of every individual on this plane and beyond. If you took a white canvas and drew golden circles all over it, you would have a crude analogy of Selfhood. At first glance you would see only the circles, but the common denominator of all the circles is the canvas. It represents the universal Spirit of God, and the canvas within each circle represents that Spirit individualized—as an individual Self. The golden circle is symbolic of our awareness of this truth, and when we look within, we are beholding our divine identity—omnipresence, omnipotence, and omniscience expressing as our individual being.

After establishing the principle of universal oneness, Jesus says to love our Self with everything we've got. With heart, soul, mind, and strength, we are to love, adore, treasure, and cherish this magnificent Master Being that we are. And since our divine individuality is continuously reflecting itself in the personality and physical body, we must not completely overlook the "circle." Although we will not feel the passionate affection and rapture toward the physical-plane self that we do for the Master One within, there should be a deep sense of esteem, approval, and a friendly feeling for the person that we present to the world. That's love, too. Remember, there is only one beam of Light. What we call the lower nature is but the unrealized Light at the lower end of the spectrum. If love can transform the wildest beast of the field, it can surely tame the ego.

The third part of the great commandment is to love our neighbor as we love ourselves. *Neighbor* means "another person," and since every other person represents the same Spirit and Self, we are simply being told to love the one Presence appearing as many, regardless of the mask (persona) he or she is wearing.

I had a revealing experience years ago of totally disliking a particular person, to the extent that I could see myself inflicting physical harm on him. I found my way out of the dilemma by focusing constantly on the divine person standing in the midst of the illusion. It took several weeks of discipline and dedication, but a metamorphosis did take place—in both of us. The more of the spiritual reality that flickered in his energy field, the more I sensed the Presence within me, and then one day I realized that there was a feeling of mutual love between us as the Light had broken through. I understood later that what I was seeing in others and receiving from them was a projection of what was inside of me. And this applies to the full spectrum of relationships.

Earlier I mentioned the word *karma*, which means action and reaction, or the impersonal law of cause and effect. More karmic effects result from relationships than from any other activity of life. Every thought, word, and action in one way or another affects a relationship, for "the measure you give will be the measure you get" (Matthew 7:2). All that is given returns, so the injunction to "love one another" and follow the Golden Rule is truly a guide to living more harmoniously through the right application of karmic law. By being consciously aware that we always reap what we sow, we can begin to build right relations—with loving thoughts, encouraging words, and constructive action—from the home to the workplace, and everywhere in between.

One of the most famous of the Hermetic principles is *as above, so below*. It is an absolute truth that deals with correspondences, and it enables us to solve a problem by moving above the level where the difficulty seems to be. Those of you who have practiced the 40-Day Prosperity Plan in *The Abundance Book* used this law to reveal the abundance that is already a part of your true nature. If you recall, the key words are *of, as,* and *is.* In the matter of relationships, we would say, "My consciousness *of* my divine Self *as* the source of my loving relationships *is* my loving relationship." You can only have what you are conscious of having. As above, so below.

In applying this principle, you are moving from effect to Cause, into the creative realm of your Spirit, and you are letting the vibration of your higher nature be the attracting and harmonizing power. Look at it this way: The place where you are experiencing the need for a loving relationship (or harmonizing a difficult one) is the point of "below." Just up from this level is your thinking-feeling nature, which is the point of "above." On this level, you are projecting a vibration of need (not having) and perhaps some friction, fear, guilt, rejection, and unworthiness. As above, so below. However, when you move up to the higher level of consciousness, you tap into the Energy of the Master Self, which moves through your awareness out into the phenomenal world to create the bond of harmony you have been seeking.

The new "above" will reveal a new "below," thus proving the truth of this ancient law.

And do not forget the part that states that "both parties must be responsible" for an enjoyable relationship. When you are conscious of the Master You as the source, cause, and quality of your bonding with others, the Master You takes full responsibility for working in and through all concerned—*to give what is needed.*

Jan once gave a lecture entitled "There Is Only One Relationship." She was referring of course to the relationship with the Master within and was telling us that if we could cease looking "out there" for solutions and devote our time and attention to the Magnificent One within—and love that Self with all our heart and mind—our lives would be filled with relationship miracles. Ask yourself, isn't it time you stopped limiting your great unlimited being? Isn't it time you eliminated all the conditions that you have imposed on the grand unconditioned consciousness of your Holy Self? Regardless of how long you have been on the spiritual path, you intuitively know that the solution to every problem lies within, which means that your life and world can be healed and harmonized by the Lord and Master Self you are in truth.

As a fearful, frustrated ego, you can psychoanalyze every relationship problem until you drop in a heap. And all the time, your smiling, loving, joyous, all-knowing cosmic Self is waiting to make "all things new" in your life. All it needs is your willingness to withdraw your ego projections, your dedication to working with the law of cause and effect by casting the right bread upon the waters, and your awareness of its Presence and your recognition that it is the *only relationship*.

With your commitment to releasing the fear and guilt and with your understanding of the law, coupled with your awareness and recognition, you are building a consciousness for that which is desired. And soon the bond of harmlessness and harmony between you and "that person" will be firmly established. And it does not make any difference if you don't know his or her name now, because the attracting, right-choice-making activity of Spirit will be freed to do its work. Not only will it bind all right relations, but it will also loosen those who do not belong in your life anymore.

A Meditation

> *God is infinite Love, the great identity in all relationships, the eternal essence of all forms, and this Absolute All-That-Is is my very divine consciousness.*

There Is Only One Relationship

I lift up my mind and heart to be aware, to understand, and to know that the divine Presence I AM is the source, cause, and quality of every relationship in my life.

I am conscious of the inner Presence as my loving experience of fulfillment, as the harmony in every connection with another being. I am conscious of the constant activity of this mind of total goodwill and joyful unity, therefore my consciousness is filled with the Love of right relations.

Through my consciousness of my God-Self as my source of companionship, friendship, and the quality of every love experience, I draw into my mind and feeling nature the Light of Spirit. This Light is the essence of every bonding with another, thus my consciousness of the Master Self I AM is the cause of every good and perfect relationship.

My inner Light draws to me now those with whom I can relate in love, peace, and joy. Because it is the principle of right relations in action, my desires are beautifully fulfilled; my needs are easily met.

The divine consciousness I AM is forever securing the bond of harmlessness and harmony between me and everyone else in my world. Therefore, I am totally confident to let God appear as each and every relationship in my life.

When I am aware of my divine consciousness as my total fulfillment, I am totally fulfilled. I am now aware of this truth, and I relax in the knowledge that the activity of divine attraction and right relations is eternally operating in my life. I simply have to be aware of the flow of that creative energy that is continuously radiating from within. I am now aware. I am now in the flow.

8

LIVING WITH LOVE

We must understand what it means to live in and with love. Unfortunately, many people can't even define the word. If someone says, "I love you," what is he or she saying? On one level, it is nothing more than "I desire your body"—and moving up from there, the interpretations might be "I desire your heart and mind" . . . "I desire your energy" . . . "I desire your friendship" . . . "I desire your spirit to be one with mine in an eternal bonding."

So we see that love in personal relationships does draw on the emotion of desire, which in a true bonding situation is then transformed into *giving* without demands rather than selfish *getting*.

THE LOVE BOOK

Even the oldest book in the world talks about acting for the good of the beloved. *The Precepts of Ptah-Hotep* written 3,000 years before Jesus by a 110-year-old Egyptian teacher—said to be the world's earliest known author—tells us to "love thy wife without alloy. Caress her, fulfill her desires during the time of her existence . . . behold to what she aspires, at what she aims, what she regards. Open thy arms for her, respondent to her arms; call her, display to her thy love."

An excellent instruction from 5,000 years ago. But can we really love anyone else until we first love ourselves? The Bible tells us to first love our true nature and then everyone else as that spiritual self. So love does begin with how we look upon ourselves.

Take a moment and think about who and what you are. What is there not to love? The body? Love it as your communications vehicle on the physical plane, and your love will maintain the visible form in the energy of love. The personality? Love it and watch how it changes to mirror that love. The Divine Consciousness of your essential Self? That's the full embodiment of universal love—the very Self-expression of God. Can you not love God expressing as you? You are a great, grand, magnificent being, the sum total of all the cosmic energies individualized as the being you are. Love the completeness of yourself, then turn your gaze to the one closest to you and see another *super*-being, and continue the rollout of your vision until you see everyone as the very Selfhood of God in individual expression.

I believe that Jan and I have enjoyed being who we are since childhood, which certainly helped in the uniting of our souls. Sure we've had arguments, but something happened during our first year of marriage that put a seal of love on our relationship. One day after fuming and yelling at each other for an hour, we suddenly started laughing. She said, "Why in the world did we do that? We love each other so much."

And I said, "Tell you what. From now on, any time either of us starts to get testy with the other, let's speak a magic word to dispel the cloud."

"What magic word?"

I thought for a moment, then said, "Rowr."

"Rowr? What does it mean?"

I said, "It's just a made-up word that means we love each other too much and life is too short to waste away with silly fights. So we'll speak the word whenever it's necessary, and laugh at our foolishness."

She agreed, and the next day I had an artist make a large cardboard sign with the word "Rowr," and we had it framed. Later the word became so important to us that we begin to call each other *Rowr*—and still do. We know now that its true meaning is love.

Let's continue on for an even deeper understanding of this most mysterious quality of life. We live and move and have our being in the energy of love. We breathe love, our bodies are sustained by love, and our Life Force is pure love. We can't get out of love—it's omnipresent. We can't out-think love—it's omniscient, and as it's omnipotent—we can't overpower it. It is the single force of universal Cause, and its permanent home is within each one of us. We are eternally the fire and flame of divine love burning brightly, the light of God-love shining throughout every dimension. I AM perfect love is the truth of the ages.

Love is law or principle in action—not only spiritual laws, but also the laws of physics. The nucleus of the atom is pure love, as is the central core of each individual and all of nature. And everything that exists is made up of love atoms. We live in a world of love, and it responds to us through this recognition and understanding. The kinetic energy called *heat* is love—just think of the soothing warmth in a loving relationship. Can an icy personality attract warmheartedness?

Love as *light* travels in waves and can harmonize situations in the twinkling of an eye. Jan knows this, and when a neighbor dog began to regularly knock over the garbage can and litter the street, she took care of the situation. The next time the garbage was taken out, she circled the container with love, and we both stood back and watched. In a few minutes, the dog came down the street and ran right smack into that love energy. He quickly turned away and never again bothered the garbage.

We frequently radiate love energy to the sales clerks during the busy holiday season, to waiters in crowded restaurants, and to cab drivers. It's beautiful to see the cold, sour expressions turn warm and pleasant.

Jan was on a radio show in San Francisco, and upon its completion, the producer called a cab for us. As we entered the car, we silently showered the love on the driver and asked him to take us to our hotel. On the way, he asked what we were doing at the station. Jan told him and showed him a copy of her book, *The Other Side of Death*. He asked, "Did you learn anything over there?" She gave him a brief report, and when we arrived at the hotel, I reached into my wallet to pay the tab. He shook his head, saying, "No charge." He looked back at Jan and said, "To use an old expression, you made my day." I think the message of love from her book did it.

Love in action is *magnetism* and draws love to us wherever we are. When we are *being* love in consciousness, we attract goodwill, helpfulness, and loving support from everyone—and we seem to be invisible to others with a negative, hostile vibration. In truth, love attracts love.

In the chapter on relationships in *Angel Energy*, I told about how a friend in Dallas drew the perfect man to her. After my book was published, she wrote an article for the *Quartus Report* to further explain the method used. Here are some excerpts:

> *I got busy. Now I had gotten busy before, mind you. I had visualized, fantasized, treasure-mapped, and tried all of the other metaphysical goings-on in order to bring my dreams into reality. Why hadn't they worked? I know now—I was leaving out the most important yet easiest step: What I wanted for myself I had to see for everyone else. It was that simple. This program won't work if you can see a Marriage Made in Heaven for yourself, but not for your enemies.*

The "program" consisted of several steps including the statement: "My intention is to be a clear and open channel for the full expression of a Marriage Made in Heaven in my life"—followed by an acceptance of that energy, a radiation of the energy throughout her world, the visualization of her new husband as a pillar of light and the wedding ceremony down to the last detail, and the expression of gratitude for what was sure to come.

She also spoke these words: "That which I decree for myself, I decree for all according to each soul's choice and acceptance."

What started happening in my life once I began this process is amazing. Several times a day, I radiated the light energy of a Marriage Made in Heaven to every person where I worked. Then I started radiating this energy to every person on the street, and to every blip in my consciousness. For example, I used to drive past several strip joints on my way to and from work, and was upset that these places existed. Now I was driving past them radiating the love energy of a Marriage Made in Heaven to every woman who worked there and to every man who frequented those hot spots. I realized that if we all were with the one person who loved us unconditionally, inspired us to be the best we could be, and we in turn did this for them, this would actually lead to peace on Earth. Now I really felt like an Ambassador!

It only took three weeks before my man (now my husband) appeared. We were married a few months later. My life is magnificent.

There is nothing that love cannot do—but we must be aware of it, understand it, and *know* it. Then love takes control of the personality and we become a channel for the expression of God's love, the one power and presence in this universe.

Let's live in love, with love, as love, maintaining the love vibration for every part of our being—from the tip of our nose all the way to the Self of Love within us and everyone else, and to the Father-Mother Love that created us out of love and eternally lives in love within that Self. When we are conscious of love, there is nothing but love in our lives—and we will indeed clap our hands with joy.

A Meditation

> *I choose to live with love.*
>
> *If there has been any disharmony in my life, it shows me that I haven't loved enough, for love is the correcting principle of the universe. When I truly love and let it flow, it goes before me to straighten every crooked place.*
>
> *The highest form of love is to love my Holy Self and the presence of God dwelling therein. My loving gaze at the Magnificence*

within releases the kingdom to come forth into my world. And I behold that all things are made new through love. I meditate on this.

As I quiet myself and look within, I see and feel the Mind of infinite love—the very presence of my Holy Self. The vibration is warm and soothing, and I have a sense of being lifted up, up, up into the Heart of eternal love.

In this presence, I find joy and serenity. There is no mental effort now as I relax into the rhythm of God, into the celestial harmony. I am now in the Kingdom of Love, which I am told by the gentle voice from within is what I am.

WHAT I was seeking, I AM. And the voice speaks of my true nature, the spirit of the Living God in individual expression— totally loved and loving.

WHO I was seeking, I AM. I AM my Holy Self, and all that my Holy Self is, I AM, and all that my Holy Self has, is mine. My love is complete, and I go forth now to live in love, with love, as love.

9

LOVE REMINDERS

❦ If you will only love more, all limitations in your life will vanish.

❦ Love is the energy that is the cause behind all manifestation, the power behind all creation.

❦ Love is the Cosmic Fire that manipulates time, changes matter, creates new form, vivifies all things, dissolves earthly karma, and emits a fiery auric radiation that lifts up the consciousness of all in proximity to its motivating power.

❦ With love, truly nothing is impossible.

- With purpose of mind, remove unloving thoughts from your consciousness and practice *harmlessness* in thoughts and words. Keep on loving in your small circle until you can expand your love nature and truthfully say that you love everyone without exception.

- If your life is not overflowing with abundance, wellness, and fulfillment, you are out of tune with the Love Vibration within you. Get back in tune!

- There is no place where God leaves off and you begin, so all is God, and all is you. *Know Thyself!* To know yourself is to love yourself—all the way through.

- Use your Love Rays in the service of Godkind to reveal order, harmony, and peace in this world.

- As you think in your heart, so are you. Think love!

- Use your will to build a fire under you and to get your momentum going—and let love point the way and be the guiding light to the mountaintop.

- Love unconditionally and be free.

- All things can be changed by the power of love, a negative situation can be loved right out of existence, misqualified energy can be transmuted through love.

- Love as *light* travels in waves and can harmonize situations in the twinkling of an eye. Radiate your love, and bring everything up to the divine standard.

- Love in action is *magnetism* and draws love to us wherever we are. In truth, love attracts love.

- The kind of relationship you want for yourself you must see for everyone, without any exceptions.

- There is nothing that love cannot do, but we must be aware of it, understand it, and *know* it. Then love takes control of the personality and we become a channel for the expression of God's love, the one power and presence in this universe.

- Choose to live in love, with love, as love—and every aspect of your life will change dramatically.

About the Author

John Randolph Price is an internationally known award-winning author and lecturer. Formerly a CEO in the corporate world, he has devoted over a quarter of a century to researching the mysteries of ancient wisdom and incorporating those findings in the writing of many books.

In 1981, he and his wife, Jan, formed The Quartus Foundation, a spiritual research and communications organization now headquartered in the Texas hill country town of Boerne, near San Antonio.

For information about workshops, the annual Mystery School conducted by John and Jan Price, and their monthly publications, please contact:

The Quartus Foundation
P.O. Box 1768
Boerne, TX 78006
(830) 249-3985 • (830) 249-3318
E-mail: quartus@texas.net.
The Quartus Website is
http://lonestar.texas.net/~quartus

We hope you enjoyed this Hay House book.
If you would like to receive a free
catalog featuring additional Hay House books
and products, or if you would like information
about the Hay Foundation, please contact:

Hay House, Inc.
P.O. Box 5100
Carlsbad, CA 92018-5100

(760) 431-7695 or **(800) 654-5126**
(760) 431-6948 (fax) or **(800) 650-5115 (fax)**

Please visit the Hay House Website at:
www.hayhouse.com